Primula the Non-Sheepdog and the Great Grey Wolf

A play for young people

Graham Holliday

Samuel French — London
New York - Toronto - Hollywood

Copyright © 1991 by Graham Holliday
All Rights Reserved

PRIMULA THE NON-SHEEPDOG AND THE GREAT GREY WOLF is fully protected under the copyright laws of the British Commonwealth, including Canada, the United States of America, and all other countries of the Copyright Union. All rights, including professional and amateur stage productions, recitation, lecturing, public reading, motion picture, radio broadcasting, television and the rights of translation into foreign languages are strictly reserved.

ISBN 978-0-573-15226-9

www.samuelfrench.co.uk
www.samuelfrench.com

For Amateur Production Enquiries

United Kingdom and World
excluding north america
plays@samuelfrench.co.uk
020 7255 4302/01

Each title is subject to availability from Samuel French,
depending upon country of performance.

CAUTION: Professional and amateur producers are hereby warned that *JEANNIE* is subject to a licensing fee. Publication of this play does not imply availability for performance. Both amateurs and professionals considering a production are strongly advised to apply to the appropriate agent before starting rehearsals, advertising, or booking a theatre. A licensing fee must be paid whether the title is presented for charity or gain and whether or not admission is charged.

The Professional Rights in this play are controlled by Samuel French Ltd, 24-32 Stephenson Way, London NW1 2HD.

No one shall make any changes in this title for the purpose of production. No part of this book may be reproduced, stored in a retrieval system, or transmitted in any form, by any means, now known or yet to be invented, including mechanical, electronic, photocopying, recording, videotaping, or otherwise, without the prior written permission of the publisher. No one shall upload this title, or part of this title, to any social media websites.

The right of Graham Holliday to be identified as author of this work has been asserted in accordance with Section 77 of the Copyright, Designs and Patents Act 1988.

CHARACTERS

Narrator 1
Narrator 2
The Farmer
The Great Grey Wolf
Primula, a dog
Moira, a Scottish sheep
Myfanwy, a Welsh sheep
Maureen, a North-country sheep

(The parts of **Myfanwy** and **Maureen** can double with those of the two **Narrators**)

The play was first performed by Stage Play at Trafalgar School, Twickenham, on 18th July, 1988. The director was Joan Scarrott.

To Rita

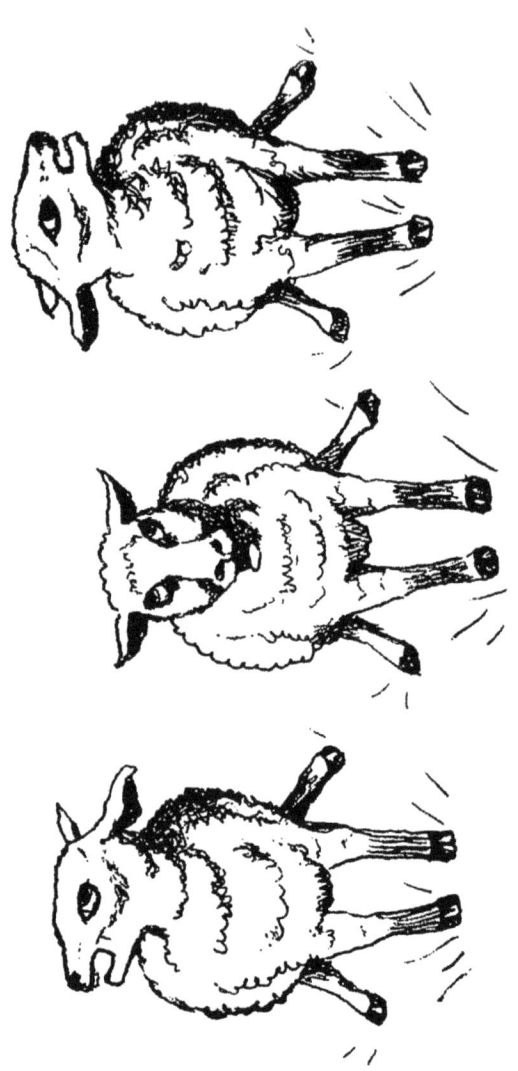

PRIMULA THE NON-SHEEPDOG
AND THE
GREAT GREY WOLF

Narrator 1 Up in the high hills, a long way away
Narrator 2 Where the wind blows fierce, and the tall trees sway,
Narrator 1 There's a farm!
Narrator 2   Just a little farm, a lonely little place;
Narrator 1 The farmer's a rugged man, red in the face.

The Farmer enters

Farmer   For every hour of daylight I'm toiling on the land,
                  Planting and sowing
                  And digging and hoeing
        Till my poor legs can hardly stand!
        The hillside I farm — well, it's rocky and steep,
        There's scarce enough grass there for my three sheep.
                I've a cow —
Narrator 2   And a sow—
Narrator 1   And a sturdy white mare —
Narrator 2   And a hog —
Narrator 1   And a dog —
Farmer   No, there's no dog there.
        I had a dog called Clarence, but he got so old and slow,
                Last Friday I retired him;
                I wouldn't say I fired him,
        But I brought him in the parlour and I said, "You'll have to go".
        He got a golden pawshake — quite a handsome little treat;
        A year's supply of bones, and all the biscuits he could eat.
                He's got some folks down Guildford way,

Who told him he could come and stay,
So off he went, last Saturday,
And trampled on my wheat.

Maureen, Myfanwy and Moira, the three sheep, enter. They act out the things the Farmer is describing

Now, you need a good dog for a farm like mine,
To look after the sheep, and to keep them in line.
They wander the hillside, and if they should stray,
The dog can run after and show them the way.
At shearing time, too, a good dog's worth his keep,
To persuade all the stubborn and mule-headed sheep
That they've got to go into the pen and be sheared!
They don't know what's best, so they have to be steered.
(*Confidentially*) There's another thing, too;
If the tales I've heard are true —
In the woods, in the dark woods that lie about the hill
Is the lair of a great grey wolf!

The Wolf enters

The others freeze

Wolf And I've heard that sheep are tasty things, and catching them's a thrill;
And I've never had one yet, but I'm determined that I will;
One night time, when they're off their guard, I'll stalk them and I'll kill,
And drag the bodies to the forest, where I'll have my fill —
In the lair of the great grey wolf!

The Wolf goes out

The others unfreeze

Farmer So my old Clarence, he must be replaced —

Primula ... and the Great Grey Wolf

> I'm off to the market now, no time to waste.
> I hope I find a good dog, not like some I've lately seen —
> But really clever sheepdogs, well, they're few and far between.
> The sheep are penned up in the yard, as you see —

The Farmer exits

Moira	And we'll try every way that we can to get free!
Sheep	Baa!
Maureen	To the farmer and all that he's done!
Sheep	Baa!
Myfanwy	We thought when Clarence left at last we'd have some fun!
Sheep	Baa!
Moira	But he's brought us to this horrid little yard,
Myfanwy	And we can't escape, we can't escape, because the way is —
Sheep	Baaaaaaaaaarred!

The Sheep wander round the yard, finding clumps of grass here and there and eating them

Maureen I wish I were back on the hillside,
> With plenty to eat and to sup.
> I'm feeling a bit on the ill side —
> I always do, when I'm cooped up.

Moira There's hardly a morsel to eat here,
> The grass is a very low grade;
> I've found a wee bunch that's quite sweet here —

The others run over to her

> But I've eaten it now, I'm afraid.

They go away again, and she eats it

Myfanwy A curse on our horrible master,
> I hope he gets drowned in a bog,

	Or involved in some dreadful disaster
	Before he brings home that new dog!
Maureen	Now, come on, Moira, what're we going to do?
Myfanwy	Yes, come on, Moira, we always look to you.
Maureen	You've a first-rate brain
Myfanwy	And a most observant eye,
Maureen	You can tell it's going to rain
Myfanwy	Just by looking at the sky!
Maureen	You've a mass of bright ideas,
Myfanwy	Almost coming out your ears!
Maureen	If there ever was a ewe
Myfanwy	Who knew
	What to do
Maureen	With a new
	Dog due
Myfanwy	And a hard time in view —
Maureen ⎱ Myfanwy ⎰ (*together*)	Moira, that ewe is you!
Moira	I thank you very kindly for those compliments, m'dears, But I really don't consider there's a call to have such fears. So what if there's a new dog coming? That's no cause to fuss; He'll be young and green and untrained — no kind of match for us! From now on, *we're* the bosses here; he'll soon discover that. He can bark and bark till he's blue in the face — ignore the little brat!

The other Sheep scream with delight

Maureen	Of course!
Myfanwy	That's right!
Maureen ⎱ Myfanwy ⎰ (*together*)	That's the way to win the fight!
Maureen	Disobey him from the start
Myfanwy	And he'll soon lose heart!

They sing or chant the following

Primula ... and the Great Grey Wolf

Moira	When the dog says stop, we go!	
Maureen Myfanwy	} (*together*)	We go!
Moira	When the dog says move, we stay!	
Muareen Myfanwy	} (*together*)	We stay!
Moira	When the dog says fast, go slow!	
Maureen Myfanwy	} (*together*)	Go slow!
Sheep	No, we're never going to let him have his way!	

They march off singing the following

> When the dog says stop, we go!
> When the dog says move, we stay!
> When the dog says fast, go slow!
> No, we're never going to let him have his way!

The Sheep exit. The Farmer enters. He is tired out

Farmer Well, I'm back home from market now, and what a time I've had!
There were some sheepdogs up for sale, and two of 'em weren't bad.
One of them could round up a flock and drive it twenty miles,
And t'other'd won first prize at thirty-seven sheepdog trials.
> Each in his way was a perfect gem.
> I'd love to own a dog like them!
> And have I bought one? Don't be funny!
> *I* haven't got that kind of money.
But I've not come empty-handed – no, I have bought something –

Primula comes in. The Sheep enter and stand watching from a distance

> *This* cowering, snivelling, half-witted dumb thing!
> She's not like any breed I can recall;

	I'm not convinced she's a dog at all!
	But at least they were asking a price I could pay —
	In fact, they were more or less giving her away.
	What did you say your name was?
Primula	Primula, sir!
Farmer	Now what sort of name is that for a cur?
	All right, then, Primula, you're my dog now!
Primula	Oh!

She jumps into his arms

Farmer	What's the matter, lass?
Primula	I've just seen a cow!
	I'm sorry, but I'm frightened of anything big —
	And I come out in spots if I go near a pig.

The Sheep laugh

	And what are those woolly things, grazing in the yard?
Farmer	Those are the sheep I've bought you to guard!
Primula	What, those great beasts, with their sharp teeth bared?
	I couldn't guard *them*, sir, I'm far too scared!
	I've a terrible phobia about being bitten —
	Have you got something small I could guard? Like a kitten?
Farmer	Away with your phobias, you cowardly mutt!
	I've told you what your job is, now go and do it!
Primula	But —
Farmer	You're out on your ear if you don't earn your keep;
	And you might as well start off by meeting the sheep.

The Farmer goes out

Moira	Well, girls, we're on to a good thing here!
Primula	Oh, heavens, I'm shaking — I'm quaking with fear!
Myfanwy	I don't think we'll have much trouble from her —
	What did she say her name was?
Moira **Maureen**	*(together, imitating Primula)* Primula, sir!

Primula ... and the Great Grey Wolf

The Sheep fall about laughing

Primula I want to run away, but there's nowhere I can go!
Moira   Hey, you, doggie! Won't you come and say hallo?

Primula edges over to the Sheep

Primula Er — I'm very pleased to know you —
Myfanwy   *That* won't last long!
Maureen If you think that you're in charge of us, you're absolutely wrong!
Moira   We like things *our* way, I hope you understand.
Sheep   And we don't need *you*, dog, to keep us all in hand.
Primula I'm really very sorry — I don't want to contradict you —
But I've got to do my job — ow! What was that?
Maureen   I kicked you.
Myfanwy Now, show us what you're made of, you pathetic little pup —
We'll run round in circles, and you try and round us up!

They start running round in circles

Primula (*desperately trying to catch them*)
    No — please — no — stop — no — come this way ——

They shoot off to opposite corners of the yard

    No — all together, please — that's right — no, stay ——

They shoot across to opposite corners

    You have to co-operate — please, please be nice ——

Myfanwy creeps up on Primula and pulls her tail

    I — ow! That's my tail!
Myfanwy (*pulling it again*)   Yes, and that's your tail twice!

Moira takes off Primula's lead

Moira   Quick, now, Maureen, take the other end ——

Each one takes one end of the lead and they whizz round in opposite directions, tying up Primula

Primula   Please, sheep, please, sheep — I want to be your friend!
Myfanwy   We don't *need* friends, dog, so do as we say.
Maureen   And if you don't like it, you can just go away!

Maureen stuffs the loose end of the lead into Primula's mouth. Primula tries to protest and the Sheep collapse in laughter

Moira (*untying Primula*) Wait, now, girls, I've a wee nagging doubt:
    If the farmer should see, when he comes back out,
    That we can run rings round his timid little cur,
    He won't let us out on the hillside with her!
Maureen   That's true!
Myfanwy   Yes, it is that; he'll keep us locked in here.
    So what should we do for the best, Moira dear?
Moira   Just do and say what I do, and all will be fine.
    The farmer's coming out now — quick, get in line!

The Farmer enters

Farmer   Right! How d'you like the sheep, then, you mangy little fool?
Primula   Well, sir ——
Moira   Oh, send her back, sir, please — she's awfu' cruel!
    She's run us round in circles, sir, she's bitten all our heels —
    We can't keep up this pace, sir, we'll be needing sets of wheels!
Farmer   Is this true?
Maureen   I just said, "I think it looks like rain" —
    She growled at me so fierce, I didn't dare to speak again!
Myfanwy   She lined us up, and all I did was try and scratch my head,
    And she said, "Sheep, you move another inch, and you'll be dead!"
Sheep   She did, sir, she did, sir, she's vicious and she's hard —
    Oh, please send her back, sir, and keep us in the yard!

Farmer   Well, I must say, Primula, I'm mightily relieved.
Looks can be deceptive, and it seems I was deceived.
I'll take them up the hillside, then, and leave you there in charge —
(*Confidentially*) Don't let them wander far, now — there's a great grey wolf at large!

Primula is terrified. The Farmer opens the gate, and the Sheep troop meekly out

Sheep   If the dog says go, we go!
If the dog says stay, we stay!
If the dog says slow, go slow!
(*Aside to Primula*)
No, we're never going to let you have your way!

They go out, followed by the Farmer

Primula   I'd say it was a nightmare, but I don't think I'm asleep.
Oh, what have I done to deserve those sheep?

Primula goes out after them

The Wolf enters

Wolf   Welcome news has come to greet me, like the answer to a prayer:
There's a feast about to happen in my lonely forest lair.
For the sheep — who had been moved to that impenetrable yard —
Are returning to the hillside — with an idiot as their guard!

The Wolf goes out and the Farmer comes in, followed by the Sheep and Primula. The Farmer carries an old wool rug

Farmer   Come on, now, Primula, don't lag behind.
This is the place I was trying to find.

	The grass here is thick — there's a stream over yonder —
	Now, keep them in check, lass, and don't let them wander.
Moira	Oh, sir, don't leave us, don't leave us here!
Myfanwy	We're scared to death of Primula, she fills us all with fear!
Maureen	She bites us and she worries us, she's vicious and she's hard —
Sheep	Oh, take us back, sir, take us back, and keep us in the yard!
Farmer	I must say, lass, I'm mightily impressed.
	They seem to know who's boss, all right, and that's for the best.
Myfanwy (*aside*)	We know who the bosses are —
Maureen (*aside*)	I'll say we do —
Moira (*aside*)	We're the bosses here, my girl — (*kicking Primula*) that's who!
Farmer	I'll leave you this old woolly rug my Clarence liked to lie on,
	To remind you of the woolly sheep you've got to keep an eye on.
	Now, don't lose concentration, lass, and don't drift off to sleep —
	There'll be hell to pay tomorrow if I can't find all my sheep!

The Farmer exits

Primula	Sleep! As if I *could* sleep — I'm wide awake with fear!
	And I can't help remembering there's a wolf round here!
Moira	Does anyone fancy the old sheepish game
	Called "Let's toss the doggy"?
Primula	Er — I don't much like that name!
Myfanwy	Just roll her on the blanket (*she does so*)
Maureen	And lift her up high —

They lift the rug and start tossing her

Sheep	Then toss her up and toss her up, and toss her to the sky!
Primula	Please stop! Please stop! Oh, please call a truce!
Moira	Right, put her down, girls.

They do so

Maureen	She's gone all puce.

Primula ... and the Great Grey Wolf

Primula My head is spinning round and round and round and round
　　　　　and round —
　　　　I can't tell if I'm flying now or lying on the ground.
Maureen　　　　This place is getting boring —
　　　　　I think I'll do some touring.
　　　　The pasture near the forest has a splendid reputation.
Myfanwy　　I feel the same as you;
　　　　　I need a change of view;
　　　　And more than that, I think I need a change of vegetation.
Moira　I don't feel much like travelling; I'm just a little tired.
　　　　But you girls go, and taste this new-found freedom we've
　　　　　acquired! (*She lies down and appears to sleep*)
Primula　Oh — no — don't go — don't go away —
　　　　You've got to keep together, sheep — please, sheep, stay!
Maureen　　　It may, of course, be my imagination,
　　　　　But I thought I heard a voice around my knees
　　　　　　Raised up in ineffectual protestation
　　　　　　　Against our right to wander where we please.
Myfanwy　　The best thing to do is ignore it,
　　　　　And hope it will fade into silence.
　　　　If not, then there's nothing else for it
　　　　　But a good strong dose of — violence!

Myfanwy kicks Primula

Primula　No, please don't kick me — kicking isn't right!
Maureen　You call yourself a dog, eh? Let's see you bite!
Primula　What would a real, proper sheepdog do?
　　　　He'd growl at them and bite them till they all buckled to.
　　　　But I'm not a sheepdog — I suppose I'm just a wimp
　　　　My growling sounds like whining — and my teeth go all
　　　　　limp!
　　　　Please sheep, I beg you — it's for your own good —
　　　　Don't go too near the edges of the wood
　　　　The farmer says a great wolf ——

The Sheep laugh

Maureen Don't give us that!
Myfanwy The story of the "great grey wolf" — that really is old hat!
I've wandered up and down these hills for seven years or more,
And I've never seen a wolf at all — nor hide nor hair nor claw!
Maureen Come on, Myfanwy! She can follow if she chooses.
Myfanwy Well, if she gets too close, she'll soon become a mass of bruises.
Myfanwy } (*together*) Cry wolf, cry wolf, the old, old cry!
Maureen } And have you ever seen one? No, not I!

Myfanwy and Maureen go out laughing

Primula Do I go or do I stay? Oh dear, I can't make up my mind.
There's at least one sheep unguarded for the great grey wolf to find —
And *I* can't fight him — I'm frightened of the sheep!
Well, I think I'd better follow them, and leave this one asleep.

Primula exits

Moira (*getting up*)
I can't believe how well it's worked, my clever little plot!
You see, about a mile or two up yonder, there's a spot
Where the clover's sweet and luscious and the grass grows thick and deep —
And it's paradise on earth for a discerning sort of sheep.
I've never told the others — there's not quite enough for three there;
But now that I've been left alone, I just can't wait to be there!
I s'pose you think I'm selfish, but I'm really past caring —
I never really have been much of a sheep for sharing!

Moira goes out

Narrator 1 So Moira went off to her favourite place
With a great greedy smile on her woolly old face,

Narrator 2 While the others were going the opposite way,
In spite of the poor dog who begged them to stay.
Narrator 1 They trotted and trotted as fast as they could
Both Till they came to the edge of the grey wolf's wood.

Maureen, Myfanwy and Primula enter — and so, from the opposite side, does the Wolf

Wolf My goodness! How very considerate they are,
To come to my door, so I needn't walk far!
Now which is the fattest? Which is the preferred one?
What? Only the two of them? Where is the third one?
And that's the new sheepdog! My word, what a sight.
I don't expect *she*'ll put up much of a fight —
But still, if she sees me, she'll raise the alarm,
And summon her master up here from the farm.
I'd better not risk it, I think — let me see —
I know what to do — I shall find number three!

The Wolf glides away

Primula Did you see something move in the shadows just then?
A grey, slinking shape — there — I've seen it again!
Maureen I wish you'd put paid to your squawking;
I can't eat when people are talking.
Primula I'm sure it's the wolf ... oh, my goodness, it is!
I only hope my legs are faster than his!

Primula dashes off after the Wolf

Myfanwy Something must have frightened her, to make her run like that.
Maureen P'rhaps she saw her shadow!
Myfanwy Or perhaps she saw a cat!

They laugh and go out

The Wolf rushes across the stage and exits; Primula rushes across after him and exits

Pause

The Wolf rushes back, tripping over the woolly rug. He stops and sniffs it and then carries on across the stage and exits. Primula rushes in after him, passes the rug, stops and looks back at it

Primula Oh no! Don't say that I've got here too late!
(*She inspects the rug*)
> Oh, thank goodness, the rug! But where *is* he? (*Going*) No, wait —
> I can't fight the wolf, I'm too timid and small ...

(*She picks up the rug*)
> But perhaps I can save that poor sheep after all!

Primula exits with the rug

Moira enters

Moira Well, here I am at last! The grass is just as good as ever.
I *am* a clever sheep — I don't know one that's half so clever!
A little bit of clover now — oh, what a lovely taste.
I could stay eating here all night — but I'd better watch my waist!

The Wolf enters

Wolf Aha! My nose is never wrong;
I thought it wouldn't take me long
To find the other sheep — and she
Is much the meatiest of the three!

Primula enters

Primula Oh, there's the wretched sheep — and there —
Yes, there's the wolf — now, do I dare —

(She moves behind a bush and puts on the rug to look like a sheep)
    Oh, no!

The Wolf leaps at Moira, but she moves away just in time

Moira Who's that? I canna see you — what's become of the moon? —
If you don't mind, there's a meal going on!
Wolf (*softly*)   Not yet, but there will be soon!
Moira And who do you think you are, to come here ruining my digestion?
I'm waiting, sir, for a reply. D'you not understand the question?
Wolf If you don't know me yet, my dear, you'll know me by and by.
Moira It's not that silly dog again?
Wolf   No, madam — it is — I!

He leaps at her again, she screams and runs; he stumbles for a moment

Primula Quick —get behind this bush, and stay.
You're much too slow to run away.
Moira He'll find me here —
Primula   No, not if I
Can help it — well, it's worth a try —
Baa! Baa! Baa! Baa!

Primula comes out from behind the bush as the Wolf approaches

Wolf Right, here I come, you silly sheep —
You won't survive another leap!

Primula rushes off with the Wolf after her

Moira I do believe that was the dog, dressed up!
So do I owe my life to that wimp of a pup?
I'd not live it down if the others should hear of it —
But they won't hear a word from *me* — no fear of it!

Moira exits. Primula runs on, followed by the Wolf. They cross the stage and exit

Narrator 1 Up and down the hillside, mile after mile they sped —
Narrator 2 Always very close, but the dog just ahead —

Primula and the Wolf cross the stage the other way

Wolf Can any sheep outrun me?
Narrator 1 He would cry out in frustration;
Narrator 2 But the dog said nothing —
Primula Oh!

Primula and the Wolf exit

Narrator 1 Except the occasional exclamation.
Narrator 2 At last she reached the farmyard wall, and cleared it with a leap,
Narrator 1 And knowing she was safe at last, she fainted in a heap.

Primula bounds on to the stage and faints; the Wolf follows her, but stays apart, as if there is a wall between them

Wolf I've lost her! And the sun is almost rising — I don't dare
To show myself in daylight — I must get back to my lair!

The Wolf exits

Primula (*getting up*) Well, well, we've all survived one night — but night will fall again —
And if the wolf returns — oh, what on earth will happen then?
I s'pose that I'd better get back to my post ...
Oh, I don't know which part of my body aches most ...

Primula exits. Moira comes in

Moira Yes, this is the place where they left me, all right —
I'll have to pretend that I've been here all night.
(*She pretends to be asleep*)

Primula ... and the Great Grey Wolf

Myfanwy and Maureen come in

Maureen Good-morning, Moira. How did you sleep?
Moira Oh ... morning, my dearies — oh — so well and deep;
I dreamed I was walking in fields of rich clover —
A dream that's so sweet that you're sorry it's over.
An' where's that wee doggie?
Maureen You may well ask!
Myfanwy She certainly didn't stick hard to her task!

Primula enters

Primula Ah — all safe and sound!
Maureen Ay, but no thanks to you.
Primula But — tell me, just what d'you expect me to do?
The wolf would have killed you — I had to distract him —
Maureen The wolf! Oh, of course! I suppose you attacked him!

They laugh

Myfanwy And was it a big wolf, with evil red eyes?
Primula (*to Moira*) Well, *you* saw him — what would you say was his size?
Moira Don't try and involve me in one of your lies.
I've been here all night, lass; I dreamed the night through.
Primula But I saved your life!
Myfanwy Sounds like you're dreaming too!
Primula I saved your life, Moira — don't say you deny it!
Moira What, you, save my life?
Primula Yes, I did!
Moira Oh, be quiet.
Primula I knew you were spiteful, I knew you were rude,
But I never expected such ingratitude!
Maureen At least we're not weedy, like some I could mention.
Moira Quick, girls, here's the farmer — all stand to attention!

The Farmer enters

They stand to attention

Farmer By heck, what a well-drilled collection of sheep!
Were you like this all night?
Moira No, we lay down to sleep.
And she gave us five minutes for eating and drinking.
She's terrible cruel, sir!
Farmer You know, I've been thinking.
You may look a strange sort of dog — and at first
You acted so timid, I dreaded the worst —
But from what the sheep say — and they tend to speak true —
I think that I landed a bargain in you!
I'd say you're deservin' a proper good treat;
And if I know dogs, that means something to eat!
Primula You're very kind, sir, but ——
Farmer Well, it so happens that today
I've had a letter from some lawyers, 'bout my Uncle Ray.
I hardly knew the man — he farmed up near the Scottish border —
I knew he was eccentric, though, and something of a hoarder.
It seems he died last fortnight, and he left me in his will
One thousand cans of dog food — and a part share in a mill.
He'd bought the food for *his* dog, just in case the shops ran short
(Which they did, and not surprising, after all the cans he'd bought!)
So starting from tomorrow, lass, I'm going to give you double
What I used to give old Clarence — a reward for all your trouble;
For keeping guard, and making sure no harm befell these beauties —

The Farmer indicates the Sheep, who all smile seraphically

Primula Oh, thank you, sir! (*Aside*) I'd rather be relieved of all my duties!
I'm not a great eater — I can't eat for two —
Especially when I've got *this* job to do!

	I worry so much about what it entails
	That my appetite's shrunk to the size of a snail's.
Farmer	It's daylight now — I'm sure the sheep can manage on their own.
	Take an hour off, or two hours, lass, and go and find a bone!

The Farmer and the Sheep exit

Primula walks

Primula	It's nice my master's pleased with me, but how long can it last?
	I have a feeling that I'll lose my good name very fast!
	It may suit the sheep to pretend I'm in charge
	But there's still the great grey wolf at large!
Narrator 1	So lost in her worrying she wandered up the hill
Narrator 2	And didn't really notice where she wandered to — until
Narrator 1	She stopped and looked around her, and she realized that she stood
Narrator 1 **Narrator 2**	(*together*) Upon the very edges of the grey wolf's wood!
Narrator 2	And nearby, in the shadow of a great and towering fir
Narrator 1	She recognized the wolf himself — but he had not seen her.

The Wolf enters

Wolf	And can it be,
	Can it really be,
	A silly old sheep can run faster than me?
	I'm losing my touch —
	I'm losing my hold —
	I fear very much I've begun to grow old.
	And what good's a wolf when he can't catch his prey?
	As long as I've lived I have dreaded the day
	When old age should come to my legs and my feet;
	For a wolf that can't hunt — is a wolf that can't eat.
Narrator 1	When Primula first saw the wolf, her heart was filled with fear;

Narrator 2 But as she listened, suddenly:
Primula Oh, my! What an idea!
Can I do it? Am I brave enough to face the wolf and try
To fool him? Well — it's my only chance — here goes, then
— do or die!
(*She rolls over and cries out in agony*)
Oh! Oh! What pain! What agony!
Why did I act so stupidly?
Oh! Oh! Oh! Oh!
Wolf What means this intrusion, this yelling and screaming?
The dog!
Primula Oh, who's that? Oh, please tell me I'm dreaming!
I'm racked with such pain that I can't even think ...
A wolf, is it?
Wolf Have you had too much to drink?
Primula No, no, I'm in agony!
Wolf So it would seem.
And I'm sorry to tell you, this isn't a dream.
In fact, I'm a wolf, so you're going to die —
But tell me first, what
Is this pain that you've got?
How did you contract it? And when, where and why?
Primula I was rounding up the sheep, and — oh! — one gave me such
a kick,
That I bit her on the ankle — just a harmless little nick.
I'd forgotten what the farmer told me, just the other night —
He said "Beware — the sheep are poisoned — could be fatal
if you bite!"
Wolf Poisoned? Why poisoned? Tell me, why?
And hurry up, before you die!
Primula It's because of threats from wolves like you the farmer has
to treat them so —
When sheep are full of poison, wolves would hardly want to
eat them.
Wolf So!
They can't be eaten!
Primula Not if you want to stay alive.
I only had a little nip, so I might just survive.

	The pain was quite appalling — but I think I'm past the worst.
Wolf	I might have killed those sheep — thank goodness someone warned me first!
	But this is awful — first I find I'm getting old and out of shape,
	And so I can't keep up with other animals when they escape;
	And now I hear those sheep, on whom I'd counted for a lot of meals,
	Would make me writhe in agony if I so much as nipped their heels!
	What will I eat? What can I do?
Primula	Does ... dog food appeal much to you?
Wolf	Dog food? What's that?
Primula	It's what I eat.
	It's sort of brown, and sort of meat,
	And comes in cans — I get it free.
	It's not at all bad, actually.
Wolf	It's free?
Primula	Yes — well, it is for me.
	The farmer's got a lot of it to spare.
Wolf	Where does he keep it? Quickly, take me there!
Primula	It's not quite so simple — the farmer won't feed you,
	But I've an idea — will you trust me to lead you?
Wolf	I never let anyone into my trust,
	But if it's the chance of a meal, then I must.
	My hunger is driving me almost insane —
	But why have you stopped all that writhing in pain?
Primula	Oh! Oh! Oh! The agony! Just now and then
	The sharp stabs return to attack me again.
	This way!

They go out

Narrator 1 And trying hard to look as calm as she could
   She led the great grey wolf out of the wood!
   He kept a watchful distance, with suspicious sideways glances,

Narrator 2 And you couldn't really blame him under the circumstances.
　　　　　So down they went, down the hillside, slippery and steep,
　　　　　Till they saw right ahead of them —
Wolf (*off, from the wings*)　　　　　　　　The poisonous sheep!

The Sheep enter, playing leapfrog. Primula enters

Primula　Stay back for the moment — I'll go on ahead.
　　　　　(*Aside*) If this doesn't work, I'm as good as dead.
　　　　　Hallo there, sheep!
Maureen　　　　　　　　Oh, saints preserve us, the dog!
Primula　Er — what are you doing?
Myfanwy　　　　　　　　We're playing sheepfrog!
Primula　I've something to tell you.
Moira　　　　　　　　You're standing in my way.
Primula　I've got a new assistant.
Sheep　　　　　　　　Oh, hip hip hooray!
Maureen　What dog would become an assistant to — that?
Myfanwy　Perhaps it's a Yorkie.
Moira　　　　　　　　Perhaps it's a cat!

They laugh

　　　　　Come here, pussy, pussy, come round up the mice!
　　　　　We'll give you a big bowl of milk if you're nice!
　　　　　Come out from that tree — we're just aching to meet you —
　　　　　Well, what are you waiting for, laddie?

The Wolf enters

Wolf　　　　　　　　To eat you!

The Sheep rush across the stage and cower

Sheep　The wolf! The wolf! There *is* a wolf!
Myfanwy　　　　　　　　Oh, please don't let us die!

Primula	Don't bite them now — they're poisoned — you'll regret it if you try.
	But they don't *know* they've been poisoned, so they'll still be scared of you,
	And I'm sure that they'll do anything at all you tell them to.
	Would you like to be a sheepdog? It's an honest job, with pay —
	I would give you as your wages half my dinner every day!
Wolf	Half your dinner?
Primula	Half my dinner — and it really isn't hard.
	You have to tend the sheep — I'm sure you'd be a splendid guard.
	You have to reprimand them when they feel like disappearing,
	And sometimes round them up and drive them into pens for shearing.
Wolf	It all sounds very easy. If I'd known that this was so,
	I'd have given up my life of crime and murder years ago!
	I'd have *asked* to be a sheepwolf, and to earn an honest crust!
	You can teach an old wolf new tricks, and he'll learn them if he must!
Primula	Now listen, sheep — I've tamed him, but if I were you I wouldn't
	Ever try to disobey him or do something that you shouldn't.
	He's still a wolf — he's still got teeth. Now is that understood?
Moira	Yes, Primula!
Maureen	Oh, please don't let him hurt us!
Myfanwy	We'll be good!
Primula	You'd better be! And now I think I'll go and have a sleep —
	And tell the farmer who I've got to guard his precious sheep!

Primula exits

Narrator 1 The farmer at first was amazed and dumbfounded;
Narrator 2 He rushed for his gun and immediately bounded
Narrator 1 Up the steep hill with the dog by his side.

The Farmer and Primula enter

Farmer	That wolf will have eaten them, surely!
Narrator 1	He cried.
Narrator 2	But what did he find? Just the sheep, eating clover —
Narrator 1	Nervous, but safe — and the wolf, standing over. The farmer was carried away with surprise And praised his Primula up to the skies.
Farmer	You've found an assistant, and even more yet — The wolf, for so long such a terrible threat Is as tame as a lamb! I'm indebted to you. And Primula — here's what I'm going to do. I'm having you down to the farmhouse to stay. Your working life's over — from now on you play! You can roll in the yard — you can sniff at the trees. The wolf guards the flock, and you do as you please!
Narrator 1	And that's what happened on the lonely little farm. The wolf kept the sheep, and they came to no harm. He had all the dog food he wanted, and said That he'd never in all his life been so well fed.
Narrator 2	While Primula rested, and wandered and played And made friends with the cats and the dairy maid And was given fresh cream as a regular treat. A happier creature you never could meet!
Narrator 1	The sheep weren't too happy, of course — but you might Be forgiven for saying it served them right!
Narrator 2	And that's how things are to this very day —
Narrator 1	On the farm
Narrator 2	In the high hills
Narrator 1 / **Narrator 2** (*together*)	A long way away!

CURTAIN

FURNITURE AND PROPERTY LIST

On stage: Bush

Off stage :   Old wool rug (**Farmer**)

LIGHTING PLOT

Property fittings required: nil

To open: Full general lighting

| Cue 1 | The **Farmer** exits
Gradually dim lighting | (Page 10) |

| Cue 2 | **Narrator 1**: "...she fainted in a heap."
Gradually increase lighting | (Page 16) |

www.ingramcontent.com/pod-product-compliance
Ingram Content Group UK Ltd.
Pitfield, Milton Keynes, MK11 3LW, UK
UKHW021842140426
5217IPUK00022B/1556